Rupert Loydell is the Managing Editor of Stride Publications, Editor of *Stride* magazine, Reviews Editor of *Orbis* magazine, Associate Editor of *Avacado* magazine and a regular contributor of articles and reviews to *Tangents* magazine. He is currently a Royal Literary Fund Fellow at Warwick University and poet-in-residence at Sherborne School. Recent publications include *The Museum of Light* and *Endlessly Divisible*, and four collaborative works: *Snowshoes Across the Clouds*, with Bob Garlitz; *A Hawk Into Everywhere*, with Roselle Angwin; *The Temperature of Recall*, with Sheila E. Murphy; and *Eight Excursions*, with David Kennedy. He lives in Devon with his wife and two daughters.

Other publications by Rupert Loydell include:

Poetry:

Familiar Territory (Bluechrome 2004)
The Museum of Light (Arc Publications 2003)
Endlessly Divisible (Driftwood 2003)
Home All Along (Chrysalis Poetry 1999)
Frosted Light: fourteen sequences, 1978-1988 (University of Salzburg Press 1996)
The Giving Of Flowers (Headland 1994)
Timbers Across The Sun (University of Salzburg Press 1993)
Between Dark Dreams (Acumen Books 1992)
Pitched At Silence (The Tenorman Press 1991)
Fill These Days (Stride 1990)

Prose:

Stone Angels: Prose 1979-1993 (Magwood/Stride 1995)

Collaborations:

Snowshoes Across the Clouds [with Robert Garlitz] (Stride 2004)
Eight Excursions [with David Kennedy] (The Cherry On The Top Press 2003)
The Temperature of Recall [with Sheila E. Murphy] (Trombone Press 2002)
A Hawk into Everywhere [with Roselle Angwin] (Stride 2001)
The Present Where [with Roselle Angwin] (Spirit_Level 2001)

A Conference of Voices
+
Multiple Exposure

Rupert M. Loydell

For Natasha Jade, Jessica Rose and Sue

Shearsman Books
Exeter

First published in in the United Kingdom in 2004 by
Shearsman Books Ltd,
58 Velwell Road,
Exeter EX4 4LD.

www.shearsman.com

ISBN 0-907562-56-6

The front cover shows a detail from the watercolour *Drawing A 2004* by Andrew Bick, copyright © Andrew Bick, 2004, and reproduced here by permission of the artist. Photography by Zander Olsen.

Further acknowledgments will be found on pages 8 and 88.

A CONFERENCE OF VOICES
+ MULTIPLE EXPOSURE

Contents

A Conference of Voices

Multiple Exposure

A Conference of Voices

Acknowledgements

These poems, occasionally in earlier versions, first appeared in *Acid Rainbow Dada Dance, Acumen, The Affectionate Punch, Angles of Incidence* (Raunchland), *Ars-Interpres, Artyfact, The Bible Workbench* (The Educational Centre, St. Louis), *Collected Letters, Communiqué, The David Jones Journal, Dream Catcher, Epoch, The Eternal Anthology, vol. 1* (Raunchland), *The Flying Post, Hummingbird, In a Dark Wood* (Augsburg Fortress), *Interchange, Iota, Ixion, Journey to the Light* (Darton, Longman & Todd), *Keystone, Kindred Spirit, London As Others See Us, Lone Nut: notes from the post-pop underground #2, The Lucid Stone, Neon Highway, Oasis, Obsessed With Pipework, Orbis, Poethia, Poetry Salzburg Review, Poetry Scotland, Raw Edge, River King Poetry Supplement, Rub Out The World: notes from the post-pop underground #3, Shamanic Warriors & Now Poets* (R & R Publications), *Shearsman, Sirens Singing In The Grey Morning* (Chrysalis), *Slope, Stagger, Speaking In Tongues, The Swansea Review, Tangents, Third Way, Tremblestone, Untitled, Voices for Kosovo* (Stride Publications), *The Wayfarer, Writing in Education, 10th Muse.*

'The Molecular Biology Of Paradise' was previously published by Raunchland online, with illustrations by Duncan Simcoe; and as a Trombone Press pamphlet. 'Firstborn' was awarded Second Prize in the 1999 Jack Clemo Poetry Competition. 'Learning To Live With Train Crashes' was published by Lyric Editions, Ottawa, in a limited edition artist's book illustrated by Chan Ky-Yut; and in the catalogue, *Chan Ky-Yut: the eye of colour*, which accompanied a touring exhibition of the artist's work in 2002-2004.

Particular thanks are due to Bob Garlitz and Peter Dent for their ongoing enthusiastic and informed correspondence, criticism and debate. Thanks also to Sheila Murphy and Jane Routh; to David Morley; to Andy Brown for help with the ordering of this book; and to Tony Lopez for more than he knows.

Introduction

There is no withdrawal from the world in Rupert Loydell's poems—alternately chilled and invigorated as they are by the contact—though there might well have been. But there is every attempt to simplify it: to have it manageable, to provide the means to navigate the cross-purposes, contradictions and wide-eyed prevarications. The sentences, related and unrelated, undulate along a continuous line of need. What's worth our asking, is the signpost really sound, shall we log the 'certain', give it the once-over, clear the decks and so (courageously) move on, amazed (we can't help that) at whatever's still to do ... to somehow make it to the not so bitter end.

Clarity of question, the most positive of statement and demand, expressive doubt—all of which can be witnessed in this poet's work—do not fail to hide the fact that, despite the poem's clear momentum, its true nature is nothing less than *meditative*. In this it is unusual. The sentences, for all their composure and apparent self-containment, look to turn wide-ranging investigation into a single 'shimmer' of *concern*—where the whole takes over from the parts. It is an ache for answers, for having cold moments transformed into reviving warmth. From time to time, almost as an interlude, there's the use of a soft-pedalled humour which turns gently in upon itself, as if to ease. And, crucially, there is a slow but steady leaking out, of *expectation*—not only across the stanza but across the poem as a whole—of a more authentic and quite deliverable life.

Art philosophy, life revelation and the workaday good-and-ill rub shoulders here, to more than usual effect: to the point where something unpredictable, and the something's unpredictable, is sure to give. This is an architecture that builds and builds: to nothing less than the *elimination* of every last obstacle. It begs that the mind be rid of whatever clutter it has discovered and laid before the reader, phantom or not: the words even, their own careful and maybe wily impatience with the world, and the contrary world that's called our language and this writer out ... Consider, answer, dismiss, reorganise and simplify. And there's the point. For outcome: stillness.

The reader need not feel alone in any of this. It is evident that the writer of these poems is, however strangely, close at hand—a presence albeit understated, minimally described. His solid insistence in the engagement proposed, and which is undertaken in the course of the poem, is realised at such a pitch it is not possible he or she *could* be excluded. The 'questions' he raises, the 'facts' he queries, bring us up smart to the world we know or think we know. The enterprise is signally a joint one—its to-and-fro of consideration allowing all parties in and granting them equal status.

There is, seemingly, no end to the race of information and demands on self. All the traditional questions remain. But this world is not to be uncountenanced. Thinking and working on thinking, for all its tediousness, for all its limitation, has to continue. The poetry evidences just how hard the struggle has been and still is to 'make sense', but if the answers are, in any meaningful and satisfying fullness, still to come (and no-one will be surprised by that), it's clear that an arrival at optimism is an important first step. And it is hard-won optimism, however scarred and fragmented, that is achieved in these relentlessly searching poems. Says Morandi 'Nothing is more abstract than the visible world' and nothing more real, more valuable, suggests the poet here, than words—words to reconstruct the platform we're viewed from (such are the material-immaterial foundations of his broad enquiry)—that we may together and in dogged fashion see the whole thing through.

Peter Dent

'Now he discovered familiar patterns everywhere, only weirdly mingled and combined, and in this way often the strangest objects fell into order in his mind. Soon he looked for analogies in all things, conjunctures, correspondences; till he could no longer see anything in isolation.'

—Novalis, *The Disciples of Saïs*

Conversation

Why insist on the word poetry?
It is the simplest thing in the world.

What have you invented?
It is made up of borrowings and collages.

Is this how chance must be defined?
There are accidents always and everywhere.

Form is unique, it does not repeat itself?
I hope to let words exist without thinking about them.

What kind of audible results will be produced?
The air is filled with music we cannot hear.

How is sound dispersed?
In nature, at every moment, there is amplification.

What is this movement into the air?
Circles of sound, laughter, and language.

Who speaks in your inner chambers?
I prefer the notion of conversation.

What 'other' are you talking about?
A stranger at the natural limit of our vision.

Where does devotion come from?
From trying to find the point of balance.

Do you suppose that tranquility exists?
That's what the nothing in between is.

What is the name of the noise of rain?
We no longer know the exact definition of sadness.

Firstborn

for Natasha

It was like opening a waterfall:
a mixture of colours flashed quickly by,
blue skin floated in the slipstream.

Children of light and a spirit of kindness
together under faded hospital bunting –
novice pilots of the future.

Your first toys were your hands,
a personal machinery of dreams.
Baby, you have changed the world.

Other people enjoyed telling me
I was asking the wrong questions.
I have become knowing and resourceful.

Empty rooms wait to be entered –
silent when you are asleep
or gone out with your mother.

Sometimes we all laugh. Otherwise
the house seems merely cluttered.
Choir practice has already started.

Slow-Motion

Our baby swings slow-motion against the sky
chuckling as she comes towards us,
before reversing away still laughing.

I waited for a friend in the dark by the cathedral.
Life revolves around it, but no-one needs it any more;
we take for granted that meaning exists.

The sun swings slow-motion across the sky.
I push our baby, asleep in her buggy,
around the streets. Time passes so slow.

I have never known these suburbs so well:
the empty lawns, blank windows, tidied streets.
The days pile up, battered at both ends.

Doubt swings slow-motion across my life,
questioning how I spend my time,
muttering persistently about love.

Daughter

Dependant days are slipping away.
You already make up your mind
where to go and what you want to do;
soon you will be up, off and away
into whatever world you make.

You can name rain and colours,
climb the stairs, dance and sing.
Relatives' names are just a game;
you prefer chips to almost anything
else the world has to offer.

This week you want your mother,
and reject my requests for hugs;
today you waved goodbye and
proffered kisses at the nursery gate.
Whatever world have we made?

Your appetite for stories is vast,
you'd rather walk than ride;
but a single bark or knock
has you clambering into my arms.
What else has the world to offer?

Learning To Walk

I pick up stones from the pavement
and run up other people's front paths.
Cars fascinate me as they speed by;
the smallest things amaze me.

I sing the songs you have taught me,
and push my truck of bricks
down the hall, out into the future.
I am looking for things to amaze me.

Roadkill

Squashed young hedgehog on the neighbour's drive,
dead pigeon under a tree on the way to nursery;
a badger by the main road, a fox the day before.

Your baby face lights up with wonder and delight
at every thing it sees; so much newness in your life.
You are constantly looking for new songs to sing.

I try to relax the muscle of concern and care
and join you spinning notes into the air where
time's not begun, and death doesn't matter at all.

Written In Stone

These changes haven't been easy.
Our cats are dead, time's not my own,
you want to move to somewhere I don't
and my mother is worried about dying.

I want it fixed and final, written in stone;
have gone back to hymns and incense,
an hour spent in the presence of God,
hoping and praying he might be there.

Everything seems forced to me now,
though I imagine things will work out.
There's no time for books or music,
and far too much sitting around.

I want it fixed and final, definite and sure.
Something in the centre of all things
for me to orbit round: slowly spinning,
filled with centrifugal fear and dread.

Indications Of Previous Lines Linger

On the train, I look out of the window,
following the course of an imaginary river,
journey across wild and varied terrain.

I'm all for places we can't possibly be:
travelling longer and even longer words
between one thought and the next.

I treat myself as a privileged ghost:
snapshots of a younger, beardless self
are flyposted around the cardboard city

as I compile an encyclopaedia of lost lives.
The racing clockwork of damaged hearts
drowns out my favourite characters' voices.

How many untravelled miles lie between us?
The philosophy of travel is a serious business:
he who rests often misses the connection.

Conflict, independence and dialogue...
What does it take to live the good life?
How do we create immortal community?

Contemplate a lifetime spent training for
a different ecology of being, the long silences
which follow our brief and hesitant meetings.

The wireless announces further delays.
I fear the unknown, intention and accident.
The seizure of imagination is absolute.

The Party Will Happen Without Me

Two people we knew, not well, died today
whilst we were drinking and laughing.
Someone's mother held her hand to say goodbye;
somebody's husband didn't make it through
as surgery failed. The pizza and wine were great;
at least we don't have to go to the funerals.

Friends we don't know very well are staying
for a couple of days. Young and recently married,
their noise and enthusiasm are just too much.
I'm finding it difficult to keep my interest up;
there's too much talk about fashion and health.
I'm not sure this visit is going to work out.

You say I live in the past and let it get me down;
and you're right, I do. I miss my dad,
I miss my cats, and (as if I had a choice!)
I don't want our daughter to ever feel this way.
You tell me it's part of being human;
I'm not sure this visit is going to work out.

For the first time for ages I listen to
the rush and swirl of myself breathing,
my heart's pale beat, amplified in the bath.
Bewitched, I sponge away despair,
understand we are only sound and vibration.
At least I won't have to go to my own funeral.

When Did Things Start Getting Bad?

Accidents, reversals and delays.
I am trying to phone the dead;
their discarded mobiles still ring.

People meet me and expect
to get into an encounter, but
it is the last thing on my mind.

The country is in chaos. I dwell
in wonderment and find myself
muffled in fogs of routine;

I am making everything up,
living my life in a pretend land
which I know I will never leave.

I am interested in the path you took,
in signs and wonders, metaphors;
the possibility of sinking without trace.

I don't feel shame anymore, don't care
if this poem is a form of deliberate cliché.
Most of this text is ghostwritten,

a kind of speaking becoming writing
tuning in to what is happening elsewhere,
blurring the personal and private.

These words are stolen, the lines
are yours. Our passports are fakes,
our documents are out of order.

Life does seem an unusual procedure.
What are ancestors and children for?
Tell me and then I'll know.

Bubblewrap me gently, I have
an inflammable heart. The guides
are all lost, the borders are closed;

each scene is lit by a very bright light.
But it's good to be here, isn't it?
Is there anyone here who isn't afraid?

Strategy

I'm just coming out of something, certain
of uncertainty, busier than ever before. Head up
to sniff the air, head down to get things done.

If the jigsaw's not right the pieces won't fit,
if our timing's out we'll overrun. I've far too many
things to do, all for a not-big-enough fee.

Publicity, publicity, publicity – mustn't the result of that,
given your beliefs, be guilt? Send out for reassurance!
Plan an emotional effect or two for the reader!

What is the relationship between family life
and the notion of lost innocence? An endless
capacity to forget, for sleep. There is no time

to interpret, things must speak for themselves.
Language is hopeless and often unreal; values
and ideas cannot give us a sense of redemption.

You are never the same person; I always jump
the gun. The notion of self is a dangerous concept.
Other lives are available; I answer only to myself.

The Stupidest Things

A stranger is knocking at the door,
to ask if I know Jesus. My daughter
is out playing with a friend. She's only
three years old; it feels like she's left home.

I've taken the stair-gate down today
and plastered up the holes. She sleeps
in a big bed now, her room's filled up
with toys; I'm Dad, not Daddy anymore.

Ten years ago my father was dying of cancer.
Then did. A friend mentioned it on the phone
only yesterday, musing on the visits he made
to say goodbye and talk their lives through.

The stupidest things make me cry now:
the first daffodils in today's cold light;
and in the paper, burnt out trying to care,
a woman who killed her disabled children.

Strangers try to convince me that only
their beliefs are right, that life is simpler
than it seems. I'm not so sure. Something
I imagined I knew has upped and gone away.

Scotoma

for Fairnie again

Short term memory loss, flickering vision,
a headache to die for and sinuses aflame:
my punishment for believing in beer.

Blow me if your name didn't come up again!
Someone who used to live nearby knew you,
and straightaway mentioned the fact.

Nostalgia explodes or fires back in your face
when not used correctly. Pain is emphasised
if you grieve too long or linger in the past.

New life stirs as the dead come before
the most abstract of forms. Complex narratives
are reduced to simple emotional states,

doubts are brushed away, viewpoints and voices
made redundant; there is no argument anymore.
Just the words and skills you learned so well

finally put to use. Music and painting, laughter,
the art of great ideas: this is the language of heaven,
where colour exists in the present tense

and breathing is slowed only to waiting.
Transformed from temporal to eternal
all must face the silent text of actions.

In my bedroom a big pile of unread books,
and a television turned toward the window
in case the world outside is watching.

That which is elusive is now strangely present:
your animated liveliness dimly visible within this
hesitant nerd diagram, these awfully useless words.

Shadow History

The cows have jumped over the diseased moon.
Now they are blistered flesh in the trenches
we have dug to burn the dead. What didn't exist
for a while does now and is making another visit.

Light changes but the slaughter goes on.
This is the shadow history of our land: fires
throughout the nights, illnesses we have chosen
to ignore. We were ashamed of our country,

preferred to dress it up in blue, white and red,
romantically hunt the past, turn up at church
when someone was dead. Now we must face
serious change and accept the present tense.

We are heirs to more than one tradition.

Unanswered

for David Miller

'Everyone is queueing at everyone's door.'
'Alone', Tomas Tranströmer

I have questions to ask myself.
Nothing has changed, everything has changed.
Something is growing towards next summer,
when a stranger threatens to arrive,

claiming to be related.
I want to want this to happen.
I wonder what will occur,
join the line of expectant fathers

who cannot fathom how the world will change.
In my dreams I paint and write
in a cold white apartment in a busy city.
Now my life will never be like this.

•

I had questions thrown at me.
The door was flung wide and
our neighbours crowded round.
Friends came to visit; and stayed.

How did I view the world?
What did I think I was doing?
Why couldn't I paint pictures?
What were those poems about?

I circulated a sheet detailing a plan
of action. They were not convinced.
Work became tougher. The words
dried up and stayed away.

I hardly ever visited my studio.
I had to cope with having nothing to say.
I had no answers to any questions.
Couldn't decide who to ask.

•

I had questions to ask the visiting writer.
I remembered him in a corduroy jacket
with long auburn hair and a beard. Not this
besuited reader with lecturer's glasses.

I told him a story about a drunken poet,
how difficult and violent she had been
when staying with a friend last year.
He told me he lived with her now

and that she had a different version
of events. I was reduced to silence
and my lukewarm pizza, a glass
of overpriced Italian beer. He smiled

and it was okay. But his answers
were fluid and obtuse, deductions
from sacred texts, magic and mythology.
The uplighter reduced the room to dusk.

•

I had questions to ask the composer
about how his music had changed.
Why the lovely splashes of sound
had become linear patterns of noise.

I told him that I had fallen asleep when
listening to these pieces in concert,
unable to find a focus or pattern
to hang my wandering mind on.

Sound and no-sound, cadence
and chaos; the important question
of repetition and trance. Every
something is an echo of nothing,

every question contains its own answer.
The music began again, challenging
me to dislike it, imperfections and all,
asking me to ignore my opinions.

The sounds that accidentally occured
shifted the possibilities. Process
absorbed everything that happened,
reminding me of things I had meant to ask.

•

I had questions to ask the doorman.
About what was beyond the door
and why it hardly ever opened.
Why there were no maps.

I joined the queue, a line
that snaked through literature
and language, between the lives
of everyone who'd ever asked.

We all wonder. The door
to the future is resolutely there:
a myth, a metaphor, a metafiction –
until you bang your head on it.

I searched so hard for clues
to the topography of beyond.
I caught the bus into my past,
journeyed to question my friends.

The bus did not arrive for thirty minutes.
I watched the sea, marvelling at the light,
followed the meandering journey of a seabird
as it scavenged along the shoreline.

I panted my way from the bus up the hill
to the terrace house via a short cut
to the back door, down a narrow alley.
After wine and talk, a generous lunch,

I found my voice again, in the cold clear day.
A moored tanker had taken refuge in the bay.
It was piled high with yesterday's blockage,
towed unanswered questions away.

It is dark as I make my way home
and I turn to a friend's book
in a spirit of acceptance, as though
being offered a gift for the moment.

Doors and shadows, metaphors and messages.
Spiritual letters: prose-poems written in disbelief,
a correspondence of doubt and negation.
I cannot fathom how my world has changed.

'For living there is scarcely any time at all.'

Explorations With A Megaphone

Records and CDs spill all over the floor:
jazz, rock, electronics; the sound I need
to keep me sane. I am lost in a whirlwind,

love all this weird and wonderful noise.
The priest of transparency is back,
ready to refine harmonic relations –

a few more nights with the tv switched off,
the saucepans turned ready for playing,
and ruin will be upon us. Don't miss it.

I intend to do my fair share of rocking,
just within hearing. Last year I met up with
two of the biggest experts on the scene,

who aim to expand on a worldwide basis.
Any interested parties should talk with
the wind, or the well-known ventriloquist

whose voice comes from the next room:
'I don't want to leave anyone behind.'
Not even the current crop of young pretenders.

Continuum

This January morning is dark,
bluer and colder than yesterday.
However, the scene will change.

An unusual collection of creeps, freaks
and divinely accented characters
are outside making history.

They used to look hostile,
never said anything much;
we just shuffled around them.

There never was any ill feeling;
I found something admirable
about their hanging-on to life.

Sound begins to come from somewhere –
an outcry of birds, the barking of dogs,
a grinding that has music hidden deep within.

What else do we have to listen to?
The noise of heat walking around the walls
after the summer has gone into silence.

What To Give The American I Have Never Met

I wish you could have been sitting where I was today.
I've learned to surround myself with people I find inspiring,
people who shape the way I think and enjoy what they do,
with the intuitive sense that life is an immeasurable gift.

Where is the past and what does the future hold?
Eyes and hands must be in complete harmony with
the various shapes and type of wooden beads;
from each perspective are different combinations:

heavy black marks with white and dark umber over,
burnt whole grain toast with red raspberry preserves,
gold sunlight and a strong wind pushing clouds together...
I watch the distant mountains turn a darker blue.

Colour indeed seduces. I am torn about the painting
I worked on yesterday for that very same reason.
Any painter knows empty space is his most powerful weapon
if he can adequately animate it on a grey Monday morning.

It is a crucial moment when you do paint over a part you like
in order to get the whole to work. I have likened it to
a string of pearls breaking: one by one they roll across the floor.
Has to be done tho. Eventually you stop trying to retrieve them.

I'm quite ready to take the loss in favour of the process,
allow language to break apart, be plunged into shadow.
Emotion counterbalances the emptiness left by not knowing,
but I do not know whether I want to struggle any more.

There comes a time when only unutterable sadness will do.
In the meantime, pick your own high dive and
cannonball into the days and nights you've been given.
There is plenty of room to stomp around.

I might roll this canvas up for a while and stand it in a corner
until I forget about it, then re-discover it months later.
Routines like this are important. They fill the hours and
help quench the eternal thirst for wistfulness a little.

An Iconography Of Promise

In my life and art I am a pilgrim
walking naked in the broken streets,
learning suffering with understanding;
every action is an arrow of result.

I have a volatile contemplative nature,
and try to believe in God – in his face
is hidden the outbreak of all goodness,
a secret smile of soft stone and affliction.

I think of the numerous times
I have been superficial and insincere,
could not endure any one position.
To hope is to contradict the future.

Art is the means by which we study
the state of affairs once it is broken;
just saying that a city is the capital
of the world doesn't make it so.

The idea of an insane captain is familiar,
a cult of superheroes is being born.
We should stand back and question:
where did all that come from?

From somebody being dark and dangerous,
funny and brave, whilst rewriting the classics.
Myth has been misunderstood – although
it is wonderful not to know the answer.

Illusion enables us to live in flux.
Wandering within these rooms,
I change despair into fiction,
pretend to see only beauty and truth.

I like the idea of people not being aware
that hope spreads out from one source,
exists in the smallest thing. No one
ever comes really to know despair.

I am making a move towards joy.

Small Degrees Of Disturbance

I am always looking for the invisible –
fear and the narrative of disagreement
are serious instruments of discovery.
I bought a plastic organ and a two-piece suit
to attract more attention and adulation;
there is no way to describe my confusion.

How strangely and slowly the world
moves along this street of footsteps...
Time's not begun to attract your attention,
to death your answer's curiosity,
to darkness simply incomprehension;
you ignore all I take for granted.

Electric rain runs down ashen trees.
Under the umbrella's eclipse footprints sparkle,
there is neon mud on your wellington boots.
Leaves and dust and birds punctuate the light,
the grass is greener than ever before.
Wherever you've been I have missed you.

A Conference Of Voices

A good week, going well;
what I've seen, I like.
I remember Monday
warmer than imagined.

I am training to join
a conference of voices,
will send and report
any declared policy.

I shall not wear blue,
I shall not wear beige;
will try to trick myself
into believing I care.

How I would prefer
large scale treason,
the least distraction
consigned to the page.

Obviously a vase
is not just pottery.
Why presume simplicity
is an ongoing process?

My Version Of It

It is always going to be like this now,
with no time to sit and type
or listen to something new.

I dream about keeping a journal.
The moonlight turns red
and tiptoes from the room...

I feel outside any discussion,
recognise only forms of absence,
the fundamentally unpredictable.

I look for the pulse in language
and try to wrap something around you:
cause your soul to arc, your spirit to spark.

There may come a day when
it is not enough to touch words;
my life will become a true story.

The Molecular Biology Of Paradise

for Duncan Simcoe

> Beefheart: 'That was an earthquake. Did you feel it?'
> Zappa: 'Yes, but it was so small that it made the people seem enormous!'
> —quoted by Miles in *The Frank Zappa Companion*

> But as to risings, I can tell you why.
> It is on contradiction that they grow.
> It seemed the best thing to be up and go.
> Up was the heartening and the strong reply.
> The heart of standing is we cannot fly.
> —William Empson, 'Aubade'

•

My summer was disastrous.
I became aware that gravity had shifted,
and had to work at staying seated.

Long and winding lines led up to
a woman whose sole qualifications
are her skills at oral and phone sex.

Jesus The Hot Air Balloon is
an extension of my own self-absorption;
I will topple out if I am not careful.

Well, you know I am a savage,
frightened and dazed. The mind
is a monkey and, honey, so am I.

•

He took us to another world,
writing the same book several times
to make sure we understood.

Each book the same journey
through an imaginary city
he had created from reality.

He did not plan to travel anywhere;
was a thousand miles away from his room,
looking further into impossibility.

He told me of a perimeter fence
with a set of instructions for
simulating the distance between,

a technology of disorganization
conjured up whilst lying in hospital
listening to a beeping monitor.

He was not interested in relying on science,
wasn't accustomed to his environment;
truly felt his strangeness in the world.

His untimely departure, this forced narrative,
seems to have finalised the future.
He was not the one who chose his words.

•

He lived and worked hard, so they say,
journeying around Britain reshaping the novel,
painting in obsessive bursts until a picture was finished.

Maintaining the always implausible distance
between the creator and his creation,
he appears only once in his own work.

•

I paid him a visit once and
his attitude was not one of distress
but, rather, of recognition.

'You know' he said, 'there is no silence.'
He was delighted at being able to project
all those sounds into the hall at once.

If you've ever seen a man singing songs
while trapped under a chaise-longue
you'll know exactly what I mean.

By arousing indignation or sympathy,
he reminds us how fragile music really is;
how finely attuned to the zeitgeist.

•

Lying face-down in the middle of a pavement
and waiting for passers-by to walk over him
he considered the possibility of praying to himself.

•

Living and working in self-imposed exile
anecdotes and coincidences can be given academic credibility.
So much for transparent scholarship!

Haven't we got anything better to do with our time
than look for dead writers in long-demolished buildings?
The sociology of architecture is remarkably unexplored.

Possibilities are weighed up in the light
of fragmentary evidence which suggests a combination
of seaside bungalow and modern lecture theatre.

•

Visual devices serve many different purposes.
It is a question not of temporal displacement but rather
the erasure of narrative time itself.

The ripples spread out beyond the furthest horizon,
a chronological violation surrounded by a group of mourners –
the after-images of a shattering bright light.

•

He did all his painting
looking through a telescope,
seeing only a small bit at a time.

Again and again he was marooned
in no-man's land, a utopian idea of refuge.
The wonders of his art are now being recognised.

He very much desired to give something back
to the viewer who had a compassionate side,
wanted them to be silent and overpowered.

For forty years his followers have been
wandering through blasted landscapes
and living on a more abstract plane.

People always think there is something
to understand, worry over the ghostliness
and shadowlike quality of existence.

There can be, there must be, and are
several events which unfold at once,
suggesting not only a confidence trick

but also a feeling of vertigo.
Do you know the posthumous work?
Slow, impressionistic mood pieces.

A landscape can reflect our lives:
we are at the mercy of nature
and the mechanics of lightning.

•

The forecast hurricane did little except
whisk a few leaves around in slow motion
at the centre of a large, revolving city
where dancehalls and vaudeville were booming.

The performers all seemed to be in agreement,
didn't stay because nobody would take care of them.
Ah, the difficult beginnings of urban gentrification:
places that seem both familiar and unknown.

•

One of the luxuries of being older
is that you know instinct is a good friend.
Most bookshops contain a shelf or two
of antiquarian graffiti and other crazy stuff.

Congratulations upon your homecoming!
I read about it in the transparent book
where air is the centre of attention
and we can learn of our living history.

•

The whole of his journey was a pursuit
of gossip, conversation and life.
He hurtled around in search of a past,
tampering with his own archives.

All of his memories, his travels and trips,
became an embarrassing piece of journalism
he constructed on the return voyage,
having made up his mind to become a writer.

Only interested in timelines and maps
he was always several movements ahead.
He had an incredibly strong character
and learnt to make a proper apple pie.

Fond of the byways of historical accident
he finally invented his own strange country.
Around midnight he returned home,
hardly disturbing the beauty and calm.

•

He persuaded his mother that
she should learn to ride a bicycle.
The result was both ugly and silly,
a faked industrial accident.

Faceless women dressed in black
assumed funereal poses and gestures
that implied tenderness and violence.
It seemed sophisticated, cosmopolitan even.

As a metaphor for limbo, a dead-end place,
it gave glimpses into the exotic unknown:
we knock on the door of a hotel room
hoping technology will carry us to paradise.

•

Walking backwards through life
after years of observing failure
he gave up and agreed to do it.

He blessed a pile of envelopes,
licked stamps, but refused to join
the community of pronunciation

or make donations to the Pygmy Fund.
He was far too bogged down to
take in anything with perspective.

Internal divisions made
the creation of strategy
extraordinarily complex.

Disagreement eventually led
to estrangement and decline,
habitual and ritualistic poodledom.

•

Now he lived his life around his family,
grabbing time after the baby was in bed,
or napping in the afternoon. Suddenly
he felt like an old man, detached from
the music and books that he loved.

Each afternoon he walked through town
with the buggy, and a head full of
all the things he would rather be doing.
He felt beaten into submission, puzzled;
everything around him had changed.

His business was running without him,
or maybe wasn't running at all;
he wasn't quite sure what was happening.
His world was slowly turning into
one long playtime, squatting on the rug.

•

Should prevailing winds prove favourable,
pilot Bob Hawkins may release the tethers
from his gentle giant of the air
and sail towards intellectual tension.

He knows from all the time
he's spent with human beings
that, although they're precious,
there isn't really a system.

Not having the imagination
to set out his own vision
he sought out a few good men
to become part of the crew.

Most were captured voluntarily
through manipulation of drinks
and well-judged insults. That,
and a lot of special pleading.

•

Walking backwards meant he could
always keep an eye on where he'd been.
Here is understated melancholy;
there is much more comfortable.

Up ahead, paradise eluded him,
but he'd wandered so long that
even eternal homelessness
seemed little threat to anything.

He longed for his younger self,
the cars and trucks and fire engines
he'd imagined himself driving one day,
criss-crossing a fabulous country.

He scanned the skies for the puff of wind
that might take him up in final ascent.
'All clear for takeoff!' he shouted,
keen to arrange the passage of light.

People laughed and pointed
as he fell into the zone where
nightmares are earthed and
dreams are impossible to eliminate.

•

He sat in the border patrol's hut
thinking how interesting it would be
to exhibit interior conversation,
make some sort of collective reading.

He wrote out his life as an alphabet,
a fictional wander through memory.
Ideas and impressions formed patterns
which have a sense of inevitability.

There were tales of bilocation, inexplicable cures,
instant conversions and prophetic visions;
his parents brushed aside bullets and bombs
to walk through the orchards of silence.

He wanted to make it clear,
this molecular biology of paradise;
it's interesting how we furiously name things:
Devon, Cornwall, Bosnia and the unknown.

His descriptions are captivating:
part narrative, part death-bed memoir;
heavy black gestures and brushed asides
which will later turn out to be fiction.

•

He felt a yearning for those summers
he'd spent performing as a mermaid
in the backwaters of his hometown,

and with his contributions to gaiety
earned a footnote in the *Rough Guide*.
Now his world had to be reconstructed.

Slipping and sliding in a lake of echo
he became one of the cornerstones
of transcendental homelessness;

as a pioneer in surrealist ethhnography
found shelter in the bosom of paranoia
and in elaborate percussive exploration.

He transmitted cries that could not be ignored
and found himself in a suburban parking lot.
Tranquility hung in the air like petrol.

•

A squiggle of lines that resembles nothing much at all
travels with ease and economy from the margins to the centre.

The noise of faint, murmuring voices
seems to resonate nicely with a sense of danger.

Military dictators, comic book heroes and cartoon figures
hysterically squish urgent faces up against windshields.

A troubled narrative of fear, laughter and perversity,
the work questions where real life ends and art begins.

•

His terminology changed
according to tactical advantage.
Just look at his dialogue:
no-one ever spoke like this.

Informal, often gossipy,
his answers unambiguous,
he lifted his bicycle from the hedge
and cycled furiously alongside.

His need to monopolize conversation,
his selfishness and recklessness,
his lifelong willingness to risk disgrace
have to be viewed in close-up.

He was trying to save their sons from war
and large pockets of industrial decline.
Woodwind and cello solos were eloquent
and sensitive, sometimes extremely lucid.

The significant movement in his novels is internal,
a fascinating window on to a romantic world,
yet there is no way round the fact he was a bore,
or that he used mundane imagery and objects.

•

He finished all the night shooting
then waited by the lighthouse.

His eyes grew wider and wider
as the balloon rose overhead.

•

'There is poetry as soon as we realize
that we possess nothing.'
– John Cage, *For the Birds*

Hobbyhorse

for Mike Ferguson

It is a new stage in our struggle for self-determination,
full of crises and abrupt shifts. This utopia was built for us,
allowing us to continue a process of mythification.

Always a creative minority, we are ontologically wounded
and hyperactive, engaging constructs at their weakest point.
Overhung and under-curated we access, acquire and conserve.

It is easier to mend relationships than publish a poetry magazine
(although this one is overspilling with surprisingly good graphics –
I guess they must be a bit short of written submissions).

I began with wry observations, introduced a new strategy,
made connections in a hotchpotch of minor work,
waded through mediocrity; then sold the show to the public…

My sweat is in the lens, my sweets are in the lane.
This is my last chance before a family consumes me.
On the face of it I have little or no style.

How do you balance hint against empathy?
Where does my paycheque come from, and why?
Achievement is far more interesting than marketing.

The question of madness runs right through –
more to do with the quality of thought
than the content of the event taking place.

Actually, this phrase doesn't make much sense.
Old girlfriends e-mail me with commentaries
and articulate what I really mean. I'm having to reply.

There's nothing wrong with the pleasures of the hobbyhorse.
I get aesthetic pleasure from that, and I don't mean structures
or techniques. It is all useful to me as I pause for a moment.

I need to sharpen my thoughts and conversation;
like the readability but am troubled by what you mean by poetic.
It is easier to remember a gesture or laughter than a date.

I spend my life teaching and reassuring students:
there are rewards for grammar and syntax
but not for this bloody wordy nonsense.

Catching Fire

English is an enjoying language –
when scrutinised in a completely different way
it maintains a degree of coherence and insight.

It is encouraging to hear words used unabashedly.
The quirky, fragmented nature of your questions
provides something of a challenge.

My friends pace the room with crying children,
generating affirmative positions for respite.
We remember so many things, hidden in the darkness.

The dictators of happiness are resident upstairs,
surrounded by a shimmering magic forest.
I hope they sleep the whole night through.

The same constellations hang over them
as over our thoughts, the seagulls flying in the rain.
New Year rides in with sustained effort.

The last months have been demanding and fruitful.
It is not impossible that fragments of history
are coming back to life, waking us and the baby up.

Walk on the furniture and rearrange the room.
Use a rigorous philosophical approach
and when I die, please cremate me.

On & Of The Page

for Marjorie Perloff

of the way
of the wanderer
    on its own feet

of the indefinite article
of internal rhyme
    on syllable count

of technology
of transformation
    on the landscape

of the primitive
of the forgotten
    on I can remember

of the oval head
of one body part
    on the other hand

of discourse
of things said
    on aesthetics

of a dark day
of fish, buffalo and bird
    on her nature

of the associative
of the forgotten
    on

of closed verse
of escape from
    on the next page

of our assumptions
of hiatus
    ontology

of invention and composition
of the final line
    no essential truth

Fluid Transmissions

Voice deforms language within its frame,
rarely distinguishing between genre and medium.
Discuss the decline of all great values.

Pixeled windows catch one's eye –
machines programmed for stupidity
pick up tricks, swap information:

the nightingale's song, the guppie's colours,
the fruit fly's dance and the peacock's tail
greatly speed up routine solutions.

There's no end to what they can find,
making up faces and names, connections,
regardless of the stuff of which words are made.

Having To Listen

Outside, reality rips across the sky,
but in here we construct patterns
and transmit them to the editor.
There was a time when electronic parts
were replaced by different voices,
but this is not the way it has to happen:
it's natural to do things in a simple way;
there are serious talks going on.

Criteria help determine what we honour –
it is as much the sound of words as the poetic,
but over the course of the next two days
these can be eliminated and changed.
We imagine more contrast with the cultural order,
have lost interest in writing, hire extra equipment
to help establish quieter and dramatic events.
Equality means a surrender to daily experience.

We tend to be curious about the transparent book –
do we attribute the words but not get too involved?
The adulterous relationship distinguishes it from prose,
gives it a lot of forward motion; effect is reserved
for lines 6-7, form is never more mixed up than here.
Exhalation of breath provides us with an excuse,
chiming is not always matched by aural equivalence;
we still take every opportunity to avoid singing.

Our search for a meaningful existence,
the avoidance of stress and the energy to write
can be said to be hostile disciplines; order breaks down.
Is there a likelihood of anyone else taking an interest?
Even if they do, it belies understanding and influence.
I don't have space to define experimentation,
am too mixed up with the narrative of disagreement.
Please explain asylum. Take us back to whispered truths.

A Do-It-Yourself Turin Shroud

Much more than crazed bellowing
is the voice of the dying.

There is no pain like it:
frequencies undulate in space.

'Do the dead remain with us?'
'Yes, they always do...'

I think of my first encounter,
the ritual of audience reaction,

the community-based performance
in an empty factory late at night.

What constituted indoors or outdoors
was deliberately left vague;

the coming forth of chaos
was enacted in my own head.

I remember images of death,
sacred presences and collaborative energy.

One could test the displacement of grief,
be aware of what lies on the other side.

God turned out to be simply
an adopted boy playing the piano,

prayer not a subject but a craving for love.
New worlds exist only in wilderness,

the effect of incantation, the weaving of a spell.
I am glad I had the sense not to get involved.

My hope is simply to enjoy the long journey:
I am all fired up about redemption.

Ask any questions you like;
I have come to a decision to *need*.

God Morning Story

He asked me how I thought I'd changed
and if he'd changed. He had of course;
six years is a long time. One day he had left,
without determining the nature of the situation.

This self is no longer a spectator;
is too stern and deliberate to be visionary.
There isn't a pleasant neighbourhood
in the turbulent world inside my head.

Working with strangers is about getting advice
at several removes from refined sarcasm.
I put together a group of installation artists
and asked them to choose a location.

There's something mesmerising about
people describing what Heaven looks like:
It's somewhere else and it's hidden…
A limbo land of endless possibility.

Then came the real shocker; I guess there's
probably not many professional God lookalikes!
He had every colour of Jesus on his breath
and fastened me to the tongue of the storm.

I too was struck by the spirit. It felt like
a man scratching out my eyes from the inside.
Now, instead of controlling and ordering possibilities,
I've got lots to do before the world ends again.

After the event it seemed perfect, the kind of thing
people come across walking their dogs on the common.
The gauze curtain flicked gently against the deep
and lamentable division between people and the world.

So what about spiritual release through my actions?
As a way of seeing and believing in the past tense
I can disperse bright signals which fall like stars.
It is difference that makes dialogue possible.

The 12 Laws Of Celestial & Poetical Mechanics

for Peter Dent

1.
Shift a few inches to the right. This is not self expression.

2.
Get your facts straight. Only lies come close to reality.

3.
Inhabit the murky middle not the happy ending. It is crazy not to celebrate whatever reconciles us to life.

4.
Know the world as distinct from and outside yourself. It is physically confusing and chaotic, but emotionally consummate.

5.
Crave eternal spring. Walk high on the grassy banks.

6.
Study single objects. Geometric shapes are not necessarily clear.

7.
Make the absent present. Enchantments and every imaginable sort of uncanniness abound.

8.
Expose yourself to guilty intention. We do not have to guess at the nature of destruction.

9.
Draw some general conclusions. Sense the smallness and quirkiness of the world.

10.
Give up everything to be here. Memories may return without the fragrance of familiarity.

11.
Set up structures only to collapse them. Lovers of wisdom should enquire into many things.

12.
Pay the sum demanded. There is a certain courage involved.

Learning To Live With Train Crashes

If all things are allowed to speak
why can't we hear parts of that speech?
Give us some passionate detail!
Found phrases suggest something
but don't deliver much around the edges;
watching painting videos is not painting.

Art today should be spiritual,
without the paraphernalia of culture
or evidence of human intervention.
I want things for mind, eye and moment,
my own transient boundaries of thinking;
want the moon, not the finger pointing at it.

Interviews confirm all I know about
my own habits and modes of work.
I am quizzing myself about composition,
no longer fear any cognitive models.
Process is a kind of luxurious indulgence;
there are no anomalies in using systems.

Methods of extraordinary sophistication
are adopted to procure the right words.
The basis for most writing is music:
step back and imagine melody anew,
let life flash by, dancing in its own way...
Horizons open as the postman arrives.

Thank you for your three letters today,
the mail is absolutely fizzing!
I was feeling more and more
cut off from the rest of my life
but am travelling back first class
to my own painting this afternoon.

Unexpected Angles And Aerial Perspective

Distant light softly beckons, falls on curve and texture,
focuses on the colour of flesh, a face bathed in shadow.
The woman has no message; she is quite simply beautiful.

Through unexpected twisting and unanticipated turning,
we have never really left... Oh, the ambiguity of boundary,
where presence is abscence and absence is presence.

Harsh light ties and binds the darkness. Open spaces,
tunnels and lit chambers, bridge the illusion of distance,
a random sequence of isolated occurences.

Let us focus on the actual process of vision:
in the thrall of three bare bulbs, domestic objects
reduce to flat shapes kept apart by thick black lines:

the difference between illusion and reality.

Interviewing Dr Frankenstein

Too dark to see anything,
but you begin to recognise
the approach of danger,
the purity of memory,
and indications of
outrageous connections;
how answers stretch
back to the question.

Everything can be
formalized or avoided;
enigma is the enemy
of discovery. We are
not obliged or entitled
to investigate the genesis
or significance of this
evidence; I am not qualified

to navigate the strange land
that flickered into life
somewhere in his brain.
Things seemed obvious
before tackling the monster.
He could sense before him
people sunbathing in the rain,
stretched out wet and smiling;

urged sceptical visitors to
invent computers and create
the future for themselves.
How many colours does it take
to replace language? How long
to re-animate a corpse? Convince
yourself you are not afraid.
Do not use the word *mistake.*

It's An Abstract World

for, and from, Peter Dent

Want to know?
Relax the muscle,
spin notes in air.

Speech excites,
breathes within
bright horizons:

a strung-up sun,
filament flickering;
fire of the moment.

Dark Shapes & Shadows

the paintings of Giampaolo Talani

The gallery as full of promise as a toyshop.
Paintings announce the obliquity of shadows,

moths circle the lamp, winter birdsong
comes from somewhere beyond the lawn.

A sail can be seen on the horizon
taking the alternative route to a hidden art.

In the half-light of the room
the slow cancellation of the figure

in a world made up of humours,
longings, shades and ghosts.

•

Traces of paint
emerge from dream:
bright fireworks above
ghosts of sandcastles.

'I think I am a child
who is playing on the beach.'

Fishbones scar the sand,
the day darkens –
shadows of passers-by
we will never know.

•

A single rose dead in a vase,
dancing figures scratched on the wall –
this is the way to explore hidden horizons.

Memories washed away by the tide
are taken to better known
and more dramatic distant places.

•

Suitcases piled high,
ready for departure,

strain towards extinction
the moment they get home.

We are surprised to see
them at the airport,

dark shapes in the corner
we feel we are starting to know.

•

They helped him to his feet
and took him to the exhibition.

It remains an incomprehensible fact:
one hand paints the other;

remains unclear if
here it has been said.

The Regeneration Of Materials

Images must be seen as they are:
Harvested fields of contemplation made to exclude taste;
signed balloons of breath and blood, works of extreme restraint.
The folded shape of a paper boat is a failure in communication.

Dogged resistance to calculations and concepts:
A cyclist races to the finish line collecting fragments of information,
a tornado immersed in a sensual moment of pain, celebrating dynamics.
An angel and a red carnation fall earthward, representing narrative.

Radical alternatives to portraiture:
Unpeopled landscapes and still lifes eerily resembling human forms,
carriers of memory and time and place, perhaps the real subject
of the work? The sky is filled with overlapping brushstrokes.

Figures appear to be eroded:
Sun-drenched nudes torn to shreds and pasted onto canvas,
an exercise in free association. Body language is a voluptuous
chemical reaction, geometric shock waves from a tremor.

Indistinct landscapes pervaded by memory:
A man formed by nature and broken into pieces is hewn from the earth,
discovered almost fossilized inside it. Crossing the threshold of taboo
gives the image, a disquieting encounter with death, added menace.

The temporary tranquility of our lives:
Burning battleships and blasting cannons, imaginary spaces and interiors;
the great quiet of stopped machines celebrating dynamic fragmentation,
particular histories moulded by man. Knowledge is an illusion of distance.

The road vanishes through a double arch:
Detail has been pushed to the edge between explosion and implosion.
On the left a young woman gives birth, on the right an old woman is dying,
leaving the centre blank. We need some kind of protective shell.

Something is hidden beyond the the hill:
A number of sofas have been laid out to face the sun.
Face partially obscured by the newspaper, I am a negative,
a house built to hold feelings of fleeting sorrow.

Further Than We Thought

We tried to make death look easy
as loss threaded through us.
Nothing, essentially, is forgotten
but silence is easier than memory.

Despite my faith in salvage
I will soon be running out of words.
We walked on the beach afterwards,
couldn't face the open grave.

Everyone was welcome back at the house,
so we went for tea and said goodbye.
It was further than we thought to home
and when we got there, difficult to stay.

River Of Breath

Already, I know
some of my clothes
will outlast me;

and that there won't
be time to read my books
or hear all my CDs again.

Past and future
stretch tight between
loss and promise,

an intersection
where topography
becomes narrative:

a dangerous turn,
hills, bridges, towers,
an underpass

all possible routes
through the woods
to where clear skies

and rivers wait.
We have drifted away
from the moment...

I wish for nothing
to change, should
probably worry more

as ambition slips
out of sight. Time
is not my property,

the end of the work
is in view. I snuggle
into a tent of words.

House Of Gloom

I flew home each night from wherever I had been
to watch my father die, slept on the floor beside him.

Colours bleached out while I was away, everything
turned to brown: ochre, tawny, mustard, spice.

Death continued about its secret business;
no-one ever spoke about what was going on.

Stumps of bushes are sending up shoots,
often in the form of prophecy or story.

No-one listens. I am somewhere else by now,
at a standstill. Waiting for Dad to arrive.

I must stop turning to see if he is following,
must learn to speak in the past tense.

Only the hardiest can stand the present;
I do not understand the word *memory*.

At the bottom of my heart it is proven:
melancholy makes everything right.

Turn on the light and play music 'til daybreak;
loss must be burnt into the world.

My father is now cross-referenced,
a man no longer in the public domain.

'Don't pull that innocent routine on me'
is something he once might have said.

I twitch and fidget, pace the field;
he zips and flickers through the world.

The Architecture Of Memory

'There are exactly the same things in a room at night
as there are in the day time; it's just that you can't see them'
—Arturo Pérez-Reverte, *The Flanders Panel*

What is a man supposed to do?
I think that faith is strong in me
but it is not especially useful
for getting from one place to another.

I favour conjecture and counterpoint,
am opposed to clearly defined structures.
There are no answers to most questions,
no such thing as being sure.

If I am ever in a state of total conviction,
attempting to embrace conclusions,
please remind me only gestures exist.
How fragile and short-lived the truth is.

•

I imagine I can spot doubt a mile off:
curved surfaces with undue distortions.
I really do hate writing poems,
swing between words like a confused needle.

Why do some of us love nothing
so much as complex nothingness?
Poetry is a simple instrument
that breaks the continuous flow,

part of a carefully constructed system
of abstract symbols. Doubt and distrust
seem just as true; interpretative biases
are inevitable. What lies we tell.

•

Writing itself is a process of discovery.
It can be read as marks printed on paper
or heard as long and short notes.
There are ways of using repetition.

The syntax and grammar of a spoken tongue
propels the reader through the landscape
by seductive whispering in the ear.
There are ways of using repetition.

I posit a world beyond measurement.
We are a wonderful paradox
whose meaning escapes interpretation.
There are ways of using repetition.

•

Experience and quotation intersect.
Whatever attentive reader
might loose the lightning,
I acknowledge my debts right now.

We are discussing the individual words,
cannot crack the code; the pictograph
is the substance of communication,
phantom pain after the loss of a limb.

We can be moved by the memory:
birds and women conjoined in stone,
swollen symbols of fertility
paired beneath blessing hands.

•

Mystical vocabulary brings
propensity for astonishment.
Time seems to run out
with nagging persistence.

Voyages into abstraction
must be documented:
plot the position of
these nameless countries;

make the mute articulate;
sort out music from the sound.
I want to insist on experience,
call this state of being *wonder*.

•

I sometimes never know
which part of my poem is yours.
The whole mix of self & search
arrives over forgotten airwaves.

I could make these four-line stanzas
quirky, irregular and sensuously inert,
send jargon to landfill and recontextualise.
The urinal might become a fountain.

Signs have a history of changing meaning:
in old maps the compass points
were often referred to as winds.
I may be charged but I ain't moved.

•

I am not part of the circle
although every game I ever played
stressed the loop, the elaborate
meandering of imagination.

I sense you aren't entirely sure:
the shadow as well as the silhouette
must be dealt with, there should be
at least a faint tremor of sense.

Observe, interpret and experience.
Notice the faded disturbance of darkness,
the unforeseen movement of light.
Language is the only thing in the world.

Waiting To Be Remembered

An email from Grace, someone I don't know,
offering me 5,000 dollars a week for life,
contrasts with a friends' poem that states
'good grace is actual   knows its place'.

Memory has abandoned the effort
of tunnelling back into yesterday:
splinters are filed on rough shelves
in the library, days are heavy and slow.

My wooden heart wants to dream again
and head out somewhere else
but joy has shrivelled overnight
like party balloons hanging on the gate.

Now my daughter has gone off to school
it feels like I'm not needed here any more.
I'm all written out, can't paint, am tired
of the scale of this city that's only a town.

The house went up for sale today.
All my books will have to be boxed up,
despatched. It's difficult to keep walking
when you no longer know where you live.

'Will we take everything?' asks my daughter.
'All of it,' we promise. Everything except
who and what we were when we moved in:
shadows remain. I am still in the dark,

will now have to learn to understand
the slow timber voice of elsewhere.
I walk past the table into the kitchen,
pace backwards and forwards in time.

Grace cannot heal the wounded ego
or sweep dirt up from under the fridge.
Outside, the garden is growing without us;
I might switch off the light and just leave.

Sources

'Conversation': *For the Birds*, John Cage; cut-up poem by Bob Garlitz; *Yes We Have No*, Nik Cohn; *The Goldhawk Variations*, Brian Louis Pearce | 'Firstborn': *Orphan Factory*, Charles Simic; *Electric Sound*, Joel Chadabe; *Unknown Pleasures*, Paul Stump | 'Indications of Previous Lines Linger': letter from Peter Dent; *London Clay*, Brian Louis Pearce; 'My Old, Sweet, Darling Mob', Iain Sinclair in *LRB*, 30 Nov 2000; *BAMN*, edited by Peter Stansill & David Zane Mairowitz; *Third Way*, Nov 2000 | 'The Party Will Happen Without Me': *Ocean of Sound*, David Toop | 'When Did Things Start Getting Bad?': letter from Peter Dent; *Certain Fragments*, Tim Etchells; *Writers in Conversation* with Christopher Bigsby | 'Strategy': *Writers in Conversation* with Christopher Bigsby; 'Three Types of Silence', David Grubb; e-mail from Ethan Paquin | 'Scotoma': *Andrew Bick* [catalogue, Edition Galerie von Bartha, Basel]; 'Taking Narrative Out of the Picture', *Church Times*, 16 Feb 2001 | 'Continuum': CD booklet, *Caught Between The Twisted Stars*, Velvet Underground; *The Other Side of the Mountain*, Thomas Merton; *Silence*, John Cage | 'What To Give The American I Have Never Met': 'Coney show and other ramblings', Linford Detweiler, Over the Rhine e-mail newsletter; Wood Bead Coaster instruction leaflet; *Rock: 100 essential CDs. The Rough Guide*, Al Spicer; e-mail from Bob Garlitz; 'Paint and Ink', Bob Garlitz; CD booklet, *Flux*, Erkki-Sven Tüür; 'Into the Sunset with my father', Patti Davis, *The Guardian*, 21 October 1999 | 'An Iconography Of Promise': *Art Club*, Autumn/Winter 1999; *Air Guitar*, Dave Hickey; *Millennium Culture*, Neil Leach; Laurie Anderson interview, *BAM* magazine, Issue 3 Fall 1999; *Future Jazz*, Howard Mandel; Bob Garlitz cut-up (itself sourced in: *All Gall Is Divided*, E.M. Cioran; *Meditations*, Cecil Collins; *Loops*, John Taggart; *Look Homeward Angel*, Thomas Wolfe) | 'Small Degrees Of Disturbance': Peter Dent poems; *Air Guitar*, Dave Hickey; *Musicage*, John Cage in conversation with Joan Retallack; *Poetry On & Off The Page*, Marjorie Perloff; *Steely Dan: Reelin' in the Years*, Brian Sweet; 'Le Budha' by Odilon Redon; *The Techno-Pagan Octopus Messiah*, Ian Winn | 'A Conference Of Voices': letter from Peter Dent; *Wilson*, David Mamet | 'My Version Of It': *Arcana*, ed. John Zorn; e-mail from Linford Detweiler | 'The Molecular Biology Of Paradise': *TLS*, April 9 1999; *TLS*, April 30 1999; *Bruce Chatwin*, Nicholas Shakespeare; flyer, The Merrit Ministry, California; letter from Duncan Simcoe; *The Night of Our Days*, Luna; *The 20th Century Art Book*; *Art Review*, April 1999; *Caravaggio*, Leo Bersani & Ulysse Dutoit; 'Richard Wentworth talks to David Barrett', *artclub*, Spring 1999; *London Review of Books*, Vol. 21 No. 10, 13 May 1999; *For the Birds*, John Cage; *Art Monthly*, April 1999; *Sight and Sound*, May 1999; *Exotica*, David Toop; *Art New England*, April/May 1999; *Rodinsky's Room*, Rachel Lichtenstein & Iain Sinclair; *London: the lives of the city* (*Granta* 65) | 'Catching Fire': *AN* magazine, January 1999; *Have a Nice Day*, Dubravka Ugresic; *The Other Side of the Mountain*, Thomas Merton | 'On & Of The Page': *Poetry On & Off The Page*, Marjorie Perloff | 'Fluid Transmissions': *A Poetics*, Charles Bernstein; *Rocking the Classics*, Edward Macan; *zeros + ones*, Sadie Plant; *Kingdom of the Edge*, Jay Ramsay | 'Having To Listen': *Musicage*, John Cage in conversation with Joan Retallack; *Poetry On & Off The Page*, Marjorie Perloff; *Steely Dan: Reelin' in the Years*, Brian Sweet | 'A B & Q Turin Shroud': *The Other Side of the Mountain*, Thomas Merton; CD booklet, *I Don't Think There's No Need To Bring Nothin'*, Linford Detweiler; letter from Peter Dent; *Oases*, Alistair Reid; *Songs of Degrees*, John Taggart; *Seven Friends*, Louis Marlow

| 'God Morning Story': 'Adam Chodzo talks to David Barrett', *artclub*, Summer 1999; *The Lightning Cage*, Alan Wall; 'Station to Station' [David Bowie interview], *Uncut*, October 1999; *PN Review*, Vol. 22 No. 6; 'Visionary Poets', Peter Levi, *Agenda*, Vol. 24 No. 3; *For the Birds*, John Cage | 'The 12 Laws Of Celestial & Poetical Mechanics': *Theory of Flesh*, John Binias; *Uncontrollable Beauty*, ed. Bill Beckley; *Songs of Degrees*, John Taggart | 'Learning To Live With Train Crashes': e-mail from Bob Garlitz; e-mail from Andy Brown; letter from Peter Dent; *Arcana: musicians on music*, ed. John Zorn; *Millennium Culture*, Neil Leach | 'Unexpected Angles And Aerial Perspetive': *The 20th Century Art Book*; *Erring: A Postmodern A/theology*, Mark C. Taylor | 'Interviewing Dr Frankenstein': *The American Art Book*; letter from Peter Dent; *Signs, Symbols and Ciphers*, Georges Jean; *Horse Latitudes*, Jay Merrick; *A Book of the Book*, eds. Jerome Rothenberg and Steven Clay; *24 Hour Party People*, Anthony Wilson | 'It's An Abstract World': Peter Dent poems | 'Dark Shapes & Shadows': *Giampoilo Talani/Imagerie Del Marinaio*, Domenico Guzzi; *Atonement*, Ian McEwan; *Talani: Finisterre (partenze)*, exhibition catalogue, alleria Comunale d'Arte Contemporanea, Arezzo | 'The Regeneration Of Materials': *The 20th Century Art Book* | 'Further Than We Thought': *The Water-Breather*, Ben Faccini; *Songs from Liquid Days*, Philip Glass; *The Independent*, 17 May 2003 | 'River Of Breath': *Signs, Symbols and Ciphers*, Georges Jean; *The Child that Books Built*, Francis Spufford | 'The Architecture Of Memory': *Art Matters*, Peter de Bolla; *Jacob Epstein*, Richard Cork; letter from Peter Dent; *Best Words, Best Order*, Stephen Dobyns; *Signs, Symbols and Ciphers*, Georges Jean; *Ecstatic Occasions, Expedient Forms*, ed. David Lehman; e-mail from Sandra Tappenden; 'Here is New York', E.B. White | 'Waiting To Be Remembered': 'Pre-Winter Manifest', Peter Dent; *The Water-Breather*, Ben Faccini; *Gould's Book of Fish*, Richard Flanagan; *Assorted Fire Events*, David Means; Museo Nacional Centro de Arte Reina Sofiá, Madrid

Multiple Exposure

Acknowledgements

These poems first appeared in *Ars-Interpres, Brando's Hat, Cold Print, Ixion, The Eternal Anthology #3* (Raunchland), *Oasis, Stride.*

Ballads of the Alone was first published in an illustrated limited edition by Utopian Compensation. *The Museum of Improvisation* was first published by Wild Honey Press. *Multiple Exposure* was first published as an illustrated e-book by Shearsman at www.shearsman.com. *Wallflower* was first published as an illustrated pamphlet by Nightshift.

Thanks to Randolph Healy at Wild Honey, Larry Marshall at Utopian Compensation, all those whose portraits are here, David Toop, Clark Allison, Steve Cook at the RLF, and especially Tony Frazer.

'The musical conception of form, that is to say the understanding that you can use form as a musician uses sound, that you can select motives of form from the forms before you, that you can recombine and recolour them and "organise" them into a new form – that conception, this state of mental activity, brings with it a great joy and refreshment. I do not wish to convert anyone. I simply say that a certain sort of pleasure is available to anyone who wants it.'

— Ezra Pound, *Vorticism*, (1915)

Ballads Of The Alone

after W. Eugene Smith

'Is the man walking into the dark or the light?'

I

towers shift down to abstract image
flames and sparks engulf a man
umbrella vase web x-ray zebra
a fragile child held still and poised
your wife will get old but not mine

time-warped doubt coherently mapped
carnival logic of urban dreams
jelly king lion mouse necklace
reading deeply into the texts of others
there is no way to the surface

hope will be merely a straw man
exposure is just the starting point
elephant fish goat hedgehog
shrewd self-preservation (legend pales)
stark contrast between dark and light

2

hunt through deserted corridors
slammed glass doors always shatter
goluptious gondola goitre gone
frustrated circulation and movement
reverse the orientation of matter

instant packaged exhibitions
and immediate comprehension
gorgeous gorget goodness goon
each monument an encounter
one more useless scrap of metal

prepared to enter is no trap at all
forms of resistance can end
gonfalon gopher godetia gong
gallery wall and cool white fluorescence
stark contrast between dark and light

3

lampshade hanging from a wire
pictures in musical order
untitled   interior   installation
desperate utopian compensation
ex-wife's new home in the suburbs

the rhythms of the city change
change by being repeated
untitled   untitled   hot-roll steel
filamented lines and textures
arranged in a receding space

a drink and something to eat
a triangle between two roads
plywood   untitled   exterior
no mention of photography
stark contrast between dark and light

4

long moments of sheer beauty
no chance of us returning
gas stations funeral parlours motels
a misguided group of electrons
criss-crossing both sidewalk and street

pools of light and streams of silk
almost medical intimacies
shoulders buttocks arms scuffed elbows
huge scale, glossy close-ups
accompanied by extended captions

the toolshed of childhood
secrets kept as long as could be
friendship madness passion death
stolen and borrowed voices
stark contrast between dark and light

5

past the gift shop and reception
ready to abandon time
casual silence   early nights
thinking about warm water
breathing into airless lungs

ripping up carpets and settling in
a series of private meetings
marriages   friends   past lovers   children
the world out back transfigured
no less than a second honeymoon

hand clamped over mouth
memory frosting over
glacier   rockfall   frozen sea
white noise of repression
stark contrast between dark and light

6

radio stations as instruments
how we eat our young
telephone   scissors   perimeter fence
find me some new sounds
re-shape, re-order everything

simmering becomes boiling
from gas to solid to liquid
correction   collapse   reversal
we all rolled down our windows
as the past rode up to talk

the king of the island
became what had been dream
ladder   ocean   orchard
the man who brings assertion
stark contrast between dark and light

7

god of the wind and rain
whirling rush of spinning earth
damask morocco sandgrain plain
floods scooping hollows in the rock
distant ridges still on fire

sharp-eyed curiosity
journeying across the map
ridged ripple stipple cord
contemplate lost specimens
despair lined up along the road

only imagine what will follow
self-cancelling perception
brocade coltskin linen lined
strategies restoring power
stark contrast between dark and light

8

dislocations such as this
explain intricacies of belief
bokhara vermillion forest birch
memories of familiar objects
dust spinning out behind

intimacy and confused love
I tend to go a little misty
emerald medina tabriz tan
no respect for nothing
all our lives are now in doubt

premonitions of disaster
travelling high vibrating lines
pristine oatmeal vellum mist
tiny flowers and fragile timbers
stark contrast between dark and light

9

a breeding-place of wind and drift
difficulty turned into song
kestrel fulmar sparrow dove
all the foghorns in the world
kilowatt hour by kilowatt hour

weaving through the debris
history apparently consumed
skylark tern flamingo thrush
high winds and pressure drop
dwellings on a hillside

I stand in need of explanation
images taken for granted
bullfinch plover lapwing kite
a passionate exercise in faith
stark contrast between dark and light

10

swept along by wind and tide
welcome guests to the evening
smoke scarlet kraft pearl
no time at the end of the world
how did you track me down?

a crowd of about two hundred
complained in thunderous voice
pink damascus citrine stone
a series of stylized tableau
the glove signifies the hand

contradict the new disorder
tortured and distorted flesh
sapphire violet maize fern
I am taking apart the genius machine
stark contrast between dark and light

II

walking upright from the forest
corridors between makeshift rooms
trout sturgeon cisco pike
portraits stare down from the walls
threatened with extinction

park the car off the public highway
is this the way to paradise park?
squawfish pupfish minnow chub
moving along the invisible road
not with prayers but slogans

dramatic close-ups and bleaching techniques
interference between stations
darter gambusia wetjaw toad
scratching and digging for a living
stark contrast between dark and light

12

proverbial swing of the pendulum
flashbulbs popping in the night
waffle warble wanton ward
a man without hands pounding glass
fed up with lying in state

back to the moment of explosion
we need no explanation
whether weather weasel warm
opposition seems to be shifting
the phone lines always adrift

negotiations breaking down
extolling the virtues of war
warrior warrant wheedle weep
diagonal movement out of the frame
stark contrast between dark and light

The Museum Of Improvisation

ten haibun for David Toop

'In one sense, improvisation is simply composition
that is heard immediately rather than subsequently.'
—David Rosenboom, 'Propositional Music'

Acoustic Installation

Limit activity, step out of time and stop the clock. Add pitches to distant constellations, get rid of known shapes. Use a brush and do something with it: make paint active. We're already at the point where the true dimensions of the project must be recognised, need to make it small enough to make it important, an internal expression like a snowstorm in one's mind. Intersecting beams of knowledge, prepared on a tremble, have frozen me solid. It is market day come round once more.

Flaunt and flourish, show tenderness, journey on different days

Pitch Pattern

It is a heavy wave that wrecks my will. I had to go somewhere, because each of us were individually getting letters asking us to perform. I didn't want to think any further ahead; I thought I was doing something and that it was helping me, had got stuck in and tried everything. Something about a stairway is fantastic, almost vulgar; ideas like these are not at all diluted. I forced my way through the crowd and tried to explain my addiction to almost silent sounds. This new-found passion is alive and resourceful, open and eclectic; has been realized on a number of recordings. My shadow turns with me and I am gone.

Vibraphones and fingerclicks, plumes of smoke drifting into haze

Continuous Reference

Scattered to the four winds, sound is processed indefinitely. Slight fuzziness on the screen is in fact a charcoal drawing, no different from how you breathe. The belly needs to be satisfied, nature is never complete. All things have life and emptiness, so poetry will never die. And one could go on from there, creating new punctuation, reinventing devotion and dogmas. You're a colourist whether or not you paint or draw. A flawless smile, fields of autumn flowers, the endurance of imagination: no revision is possible. The alternative is frightening.

Media ghost, cybernetics, obvious signature

Sirens

A few months ago, you surprised me, awake in the darkest night. Soundbites brought on the jitters, your sarcasm nonsensical rhymes. Beginning to find my way in the dark I imagined the headlines, interviews, headlines, reviews. We seem to live in only one room now, writing mainly for other voices. The tape recorder offers terrible loss and reminders of pleasures gone. All of it seems distant; stars are everywhere.

Broken glass, monotonous language, folded treasures taking flight

At Home Somehow

Tomorrow is the soundtrack of our times. Sunrise first and sunset last: pictures of the sky lit by fire. In the toyshop, the breathing of parents pooling their resources. In the window, paradox hiding behind a fountain; one of my most frugal pieces. Elements found here previously existed in my notebook; the confessional poet cannot bear to be alone.

Background drone, disbelief, equipment filling up the floor

Spittle & Talk

Dense noise textures: the shock has burnt through the audience, has had a huge effect on time. It may illuminate a dark passage, may bring consolation and grief together in the charts. The trick lies in the mixing. Give me your approval, proffer flowered affection, keep the illusion alive. A man steps forward from the crowd, looks around, and safely boards his ship. He never wants to be near that song again.

Secret password, focus, a single drop of water

Soundtrack

It is an overboard piece. Dragged from the water, she didn't dare to open her hands. Landscape is still a place for discovery, whatever world you inhabit. The house which I grew up in is in the simplest picture book. And when we walked round the corner, along the circumference of an enormous room, the whale's great back in the silent sea. Dragged to the water, the music ends as a statement of grief.

Emphasis, strange bedfellows, children leafing through a shipwrecked book

Anger (For String Quartet)

Places are simultaneously real and metaphoric. Listen to my brother playing, inhabiting a world of his own creation; the hill's resolute plainness seems a rebuke to the making of it. I have an image of someone smashing windows with the curtains drawn, it's always the fool that finds the treasure. Pack your things and confess it was loneliness that killed him: he never played a note. Who cares about the security of the house?

Conjecture, buckets filled with gravel, clandestine and stolen

Promenade

The score left an opening through dreams into empty space; she simply dropped a stone. Showing was just pointing; any influences could be electronically processed, then magnified and sold. The blurred story continues, developed and strengthened, given an imaginative title. Ripples move out, crossing the line between looking for fossils and listening to birds, an ornithology rather than a band. All you have to do is push one button then relax.

Play the book, unpublished theory, less experienced musicians

Sonic Boom

Face down in the sun. Two voices divide into four and then eight. It is easy to have foolish thoughts, to speculate the process is complete. All you require is a brief report, the police will do the rest. Confucius would say that music is the most important part of government; I've always liked humour and been attracted to the bizarre. There is no music now in all of the imagined land.

Shadow of a running man, bubbles in the air, a museum of improvisation

Multiple Exposure (Ballads of the Alone 2)

after Aaron Siskind

'It has to do basically with bringing order into our life.'

1

asphalt sparkles with energy
on the shoulder of the highway
insipid plankton thermal hoof
inner tensions transform the image
swing and tilt between two planes

a fascination with fragmentation
language and lettering on city walls
trumpet weasel electric poise
it looks like it says something
you never know just what it means

pleasures and terrors of levitation
opposing forces held
lark denial vital sources
we can only see the shadows
balance of time as well as form

2

the exhilaration of uncertainty
slow shutter speeds achieving blur
turret nostril gugtupper wilt
a reflection of basic duality
only implied by surface

delicately repeating shadows
falling across an unlocked door
buzzer velvet diffident swoosh
all my possessions in a suitcase
stone doorstep become a home

reality seen as dappled abstraction
wounds and healing, experience, age
pilchard goldsmith billabong beak
vital symbols of life and change
balance of time as well as form

3

memory's continuous imagination
more than ever I feel alone
definition plummet grimace cleave
things we try to forget are there
laid out cold on the front lawn

a certain corner of the dancefloor
the missing centre of the sign
ovary frankness forensic drift
how does it feel to hit the wall?
the rest of the body is worn away

last drops squeezed from a dirty rag
betrayal of the people
ostrich acquaintance coracle launch
doors and windows flung wide open
balance of time as well as form

4

private feeling or actual happening
welcoming batch of diverse events
serenity fissure percussion wrap
impossible questions well worth asking
the hobgoblin of little minds

find the asylum before it shuts
our factories are closing down
incidence binomial puncture twist
there was all the time in the world
past is now a lump in the throat

we all crave the caress of the voice
desire approval of the ear
waterfall slipper wheelbarrow tryst
somewhere else just out of sight
balance of time as well as form

5

I could show you my passport
how to get to there from here
tangent router herring slump
the idea of a map or songline
truth in circumference and in form

criss-cross and open-endedness
nothing left for us to find
ubiquitous mallard vibration spoon
cutting back and weeding out
we are forever walking

man made a journey to the stars
I have not gone so far
admittance walnut muck deceit
mysteries, dreams and superstition
balance of time as well as form

6

industry working around the clock
how drab and sham it gets
luminous urge adhesion chord
history is fascinating in itself
explained past provokes our doubt

sound quality of imagination
posthumous blueprint for applause
nutrition banter fillet tern
distant view of zinc-grey waves
a window into another time

I am complicit in betrayal
dazzled by acts of being kind
wingtip incursion hypnosis proof
assert the value of the present
balance of time as well as form

7

being inspired turning a corner
whatever suits expressive needs
snorkel tunic social pike
muffled in our waterproofs
our fires have been extinguished

incidental friends and furniture
the slow advance of science
cordial extremity sealant clip
community of enlightenment
cosmic tunes and heavy tax

an older more essential world
threshold of heaven reached
intransigent basic contortion melt
ceaseless dance of ambiguity
balance of time as well as form

8

cooking breakfast over a fire
further from home than you
helical compassion disqualified hound
suburb to the vanishing point
transient images of our town

here there is no sodium haze
the evening sky glows green
invisible marmoset daffodil proof
part of a large invisible system
devils with snakes for hair

the aeroplane falls slowly
through a tangle of briars
cerebral trouser palladium milk
sudden shimmer of light and leaves
balance of time as well as form

9

another set of ruined buildings
ghosts of structures such as these
inculpate query sausage tilt
bridges, girders, lines and chains
a peculiar perspective

light brown coat in case of rain
a favourite of my father's
cornflake wrestler resurgence monk
drifting fog among dripping pines
living worlds of mutual trust

a sort of shrinking into life
phantom pains within my chest
volcanic upright belligerent jump
sheets of paper blackened with print
balance of time as well as form

10

hundreds of forgotten pictures
sometimes layered deep
exclamation register irrigate chime
overheard rooms empty of noise
transparent moments such as these

love shows itself minute by minute
in ways that are easy to doubt
inverse armature liquorice cheese
alcohol has dulled its progress
formation dancing in the tide

the midday sun is strengthening
gravity become too much
cucumber traffic fearless grill
there is only absence in the world
balance of time as well as form

II

a long night of unsettled weather
gulls above rise high and scream
spider illusion crocodile scar
lighter patch on hill's steep slope
clouds ahead of a silent storm

stood there in a kind of trance
minimal movement and pressure
sidegarnet filcher horology graft
stumbling over secret words
remembering my real name

the backs of terraced houses
girls dancing in the street
persecute porcupine salient cheek
prettily built and fully glazed
balance of time as well as form

12

places we'll never visit again
a small trapdoor in the floor
miltweeker prophecy indulgence clamp
echoes cancel each other out
water gone quiet in pools

inside talking about money
outside shouting at snow
navigate backbill repertoire lurch
elevator doors beginning to close
chance ringing of church bells

he takes that rucksack everywhere
presses the shutter release
morphism physics nylon savant
learn to love light as well as dark
balance of time as well as form

Portrait Gallery

A Portrait of Scott T.

He leaves us to listen, is so dazzling in himself the target disappears. Differences may not matter very much, he reasons; a whole series of themes begin to fit together. He keeps at his work regardless of attention, sees the social stuff is more serious than sweets and sneakers, acts as though nothing has happened. Filling the fruitbowl, he moves away from risk, is now an extended photo session. He would be a man exploring connections, transforming a dark universe to smiling synthetic bliss.

Cyclone fence, chocolate grinder, tape recorder on fast forward

A Portrait of Andy B.

Continuous metal windows. He is structured exclusively by syntax and the unkind composition of long poems, walks directly from the generative sentence to the lyric. He would never look at a hairy jumper, prefers an alienated ramble among the wretched of the earth. When the theme music starts he is up and gone, preferring solo passage. What begins as pure speech ends as pure sound, his interior space flows out into the surrounding landscape. He has never come home from school, prefers spiders close up to writing on a blackboard. A car pulls up to an empty lot.

A shift of timbre, sand poured on paper, two friends arm in arm

A Portrait of Dorothy N.

Something has pushed her into permanent question. She is a diverse community, holds out her hands to you but has never been properly introduced. Turning off all the lights, she lets us assume no-one is home; we must not let her get away with it. Emotion and technique co-operate, confess to expertise. Perceiving words, she renders them valuable: everything becomes a gift, free for all; a theatre of memory and direct experience, dialogue and silent response.

Storm clouds, long flight of stairs, light bulb painted black

A Portrait of Sheila M.

She lives an easy life, upbeat and careful; wants people in her space, laughing, breathing, words ringing in their ears. Language has an intuitive relationship with her, the process looks set to continue. She sings out loud, tiptoes timidly around the edges of lunchtime, finishes her decaff and sees what is going to happen. Word is her natural habitat, a continual overlapping of sound and image. Off balance, perhaps, though the last line fulfils.

Anticipatory tension, mimetic sense, disguise

A Portrait of Roselle A.

She is rehearsing not being brilliant, got into making because she loves listening to potential. Is a feminine protest against anger and bitterness and regret. Now she is in language, is easy and familiar as she enters into self (though the boundaries are less defined). Truth is foregrounded, elemental forces dance; what is inside the soul and mind is what is important. She stirs me strangely, challenges and warms. Now I know there are other possibilities in the way of putting things together.

Argument, prayer, song and poetry

A Portrait of Robert J.

He is imagining new thought, giving us glimpses of reconceived realities. Rather than self-parody, he foregrounds confusion and uncoordination; is deceptively fun to meet. He wants simply to be adopted by chaos, has always functioned as an antidote to order. Puffing steam trains, shapeless wooden boxes and tatty leatherbound things punctuate the space between genres: in these less populous regions the odds are in his favour, for there are no nooks and crannies, he does not have to wash wellington boots or undertake publicity tours. He is genuinely hopeful, right up until the last minute, that he fits into our world. He has no absolutes.

Upside down neon signs, two hands shaking, trees blowing in the wind

A Portrait of Philip R.

Small inflections. The instrument is wired to memory, the components generate new sounds. He is potentially poetic, wishes to ensure the continuous renewal of music. Borrowing thought, he is never predictable, doesn't like looking down. Flickering film, sunshine and others' brainwaves form a drawing of his world. He is not interested in concepts of originality, prefers to learn and unlock doors, hoping for ecstasy and eloquence. Frequently wise, he often comes to rest in happening and complexity, having rebuilt the city in miniature.

Wires on the floor, full ashtray, ball rolling on metal tracks

Self Portrait

He plans to become wide-open, accessible and reciprocating; his search is never-ending. Interested in several sounds at once, he is gradually withdrawing into the museum of improvisation, stripped of all certainty and subject. The tape runs forward and backwards, he reaches out to touch structure, starts a relationship with simplicity. He has no way of explaining the lines on the canvas, the arrows on the floor, the small pile of change assembled by his bed. He loves to subvert what follows or proceeds, has a different notion of time, embraces metaphorical distortion; knows there are no second chances.

Impulse and inquiry, the wooing of intuitive states

Wallflower
(Ballads of the Alone 3)

after Ralph Eugene Meatyard
and Deborah Turbeville

'my pictures walk a tightrope'

I

painting declared to be dead
subject almost accidental
eggplant consumption almanac duke
found to be alive again
deserving of attention

sidelong or lazy glances
acts of understatement
charlie samba intestine towel
red fingernails grown too long
eroticize the landscape

visible elements of time
geometric stylization
platinum furbish suntan yowl
all the people have now gone
memory of something seen

2

I don't have a camera
I want to make a film
talisman agate waddle cope
in the greenhouse frizz and perm
peeling paint and ancient stone

crumpled fabric on the floor
suggests a woman's height
anglican distillate cranberry snick
absurd game of hide-and-seek
a kind of invitation

images you want to keep
vapourized by sunlight
airline reversion enzyme blurt
pack up and get out of here
memory of something seen

3

blue light   snow light   twins and trees
recurrent syncopations
rectory sickroom sideband talk
blaze of bracken   pleats and tucks
autumnal oatmeal clothing

scratchy prints and greasy lens
drapes on someone's sofa
whitlock darkle mustang crop
black kohl eyes and hennaed hair
cardboard boxes tied with string

velvet dresses dragged through dirt
mannequins and models
winter keyhole downgrade prim
soft focus view through broken glass
memory of something seen

4

striking features   drafty halls
beauty in new clothing
avalanche   resin   cubbyhole   boot
excuse me I don't want to dance
desire half understood

bodies in the freezer
held in contorted poses
magpie   supine   baseline   wheel
conspiracy may be afoot
amnesia and neuroses

a kind of moody restlessness
more fiction than fact
buried   rowboat   buckhorn   mate
absence to be grateful for
memory of something seen

5

chew your fingers   suck your hair
pose against the wall
elaborate   giddy   denizen   stale
frozen space   erotica
stay hidden in your room

muted understatement
no image of herself
gangster   bonnet   schoolgirl   roof
shattered mirrors   silver shards
reflections of contempt

beautiful puppet features
needing a name or place
paperweight   invite   contaminate   book
strangers from invented time
memory of something seen

6

jump-rope songs and bawdy rhymes
strange machines and flying saucers
feather continuum decorate swing
a magic circle drawn in ink
hush of a dark window

people sent around the world
their own fantastic spaces
spatterdock token mahogany jibe
emerging into light too harsh
clutching the past about them

distant music   ringing bells
a little out of tune
mandrake arcade forestry din
soundtrack of angelic song
memory of something seen

7

monuments and steel towers
strange idea of a city
deadlock participant contingent swarm
traffic patterns eyes and ears
impromptu dance and theatre

apologetic prayer flags
hung on flimsy sticks
utopian addict breastplate rune
tomorrow is a one-way trip
the past another day

dark stripes tyre tracks in the snow
curved steps in hard-edged shadow
candlelight vandal melamine state
making it up as you go along
memory of something seen

8

isolated mausoleum
rent always months behind
comeback tussle playmate breeze
look at the corpse in the cold
and wonder where you've been

repetition and repeat
life's low grade mechanics
floodlight turtle dreamboat wave
half-hearted prayer   posture of grace
belief's elastic creed

hollow-eyed skull in the cupboard
a template for death when it comes
cockroach proscenium confiscate brawl
the life you save may be your own
memory of something seen

9

fantasy is self-comfort
waiting outside the door
vector departure masquerade fugue
one old hand gripping another
love no longer our home

this is no amusement park
just the same old skin
signpost homeland ambassador squint
over the island into the river
assassination team

out of my mind on photography
not knowing what to do
bakelite tattoo carrion wave
the creative action of decay
memory of something seen

10

remember the stranger I never met
his mock-confessional tone
fibrosis pigeon undulate clone
walking the streets for no good reason
day unfolding like a dream

flirting with likeable images
only one passion back then
waxwork mouthful headland page
the camera a way to hold conversation
breath and wind the very same thing

further along the spiritual path
speaking only in your own words
toothpaste beachcomb embellishment tang
choose one direction or another
memory of something seen

II

squinting at the morning sun
everything in flames
soprano bypass petroleum realm
phone numbers safe in my pocket
light floods along the hall

shooting at others to stay alive
always on the wrong side
paradigm centaur lumbar gloat
every day the fat guard speaks
I forget I am never alone

the emotional release of mourning
the power to make death go away
curlicue shoofly cholera drop
a chance to tell a great story
memory of something seen

12

magical textures of light engross
firefly showers sparkle and gleam
tilt procession acetate spade
I am practising improvisation
breaking all my own rules

the voiceless with drum and banners
lies and slogans on tv
conserve confessor padlock lathe
a man alone in a reinforced cage
collaging quotes and screams

dying here would not be useful
you're too good-looking for that
firepower azimuth hypocrite fact
the pain of trying to retrieve the past
memory of something seen

Sources

'Ballads of the Alone': *Bookforum*, Fall 2001; *A Friend of the Earth*, T.C. Boyle; *Performance Art*, RoseLee Goldberg; 'Through the Crash Barrier', L.J. Hurst; *Minimalism*, ed. James Meyer; *Beyond the Frozen Sea*, Edwin Mickleburgh; *Another Roadside Attraction*, Tom Robbins; *W. Eugene Smith* [Phaidon 55 monograph]; *Joel-Peter Witkin* [Phaidon 55 monograph]; *Arcana: musicians on Music*, ed. John Zorn. | 'Museum of Improvisation': Interview with Milton Resnick, *Nielsen Gallery News*, April 2000; CD booklet, *Ohm: the early gurus of electronic music; pixel juice*, Jeff Noon; *The Weather of Words*, Mark Strand; *Arcana: musicians on music*, ed. John Zorn | 'Multiple Exposure': letter from Clark Allison; *Ars-Interpres #1; Don't Ask Me What I Mean*, eds. Clare Brown and Don Paterson; *The Cryptographer*, Tobias Hill; *Sea Room*, Adam Nicolson; *Austerlitz*, W.G. Sebald; *Aaron Siskind* [Phaidon 55 monograph]; *Heaven*, Peter Stanford; *Ocean of Sound*, David Toop; music lists by wetbicycleclappersoup | 'Wallflower': *Fools Rush In*, Bill Carter; *JG Ballard*, Michael Delville; 'Where have all the people gone?', Michael Glover, *The Independent*, 9 January 2004; *Motherless Brooklyn*, Jonathan Lethem; *The Second Coming*, Antony Lopez; *Ralph Eugene Meatyard* [Phaidon 55 monograph]; *Ezra Pound. The Pisan Cantos*, ed. Richard Sieburth; *Think of the Self Speaking. Harry Smith – Selected Interviews; Wallflower*, Deborah Turbeville.

www.ingramcontent.com/pod-product-compliance
Lightning Source LLC
Chambersburg PA
CBHW032052150426
43194CB00006B/509
9780907562566